T0065109

# THE HAPPY
# Empath's
## LITTLE BOOK OF
# Affirmations

## MINDFUL MANTRAS FOR
## DAILY SELF-CARE

### STEPHANIE JAMESON

ULYSSES PRESS

Published by:
ULYSSES PRESS
PO Box 3440
Berkeley, CA 94703
www.ulyssespress.com

ISBN: 978-1-64604-080-3
Library of Congress Control Number: 2020935551

Printed in the United States by Versa Press
2 4 6 8 10 9 7 5 3

Acquisitions editor: Casie Vogel
Managing editor: Claire Chun
Editor: Renee Rutledge
Proofreader: Kathy Kaiser
Front cover design: Justin Shirley
Cover art: © Jana M/shutterstock.com
Interior design: Jake Flaherty
Interior art: © shutterstock.com

For little Stephanie.

I've got your back, lets do this…

# INTRODUCTION

## What is an empath?

An empath has the ability to feel or sense what someone else has felt or is feeling, even when that emotion is not being expressed. An empath then tends to take on that emotion and process it themselves. Born with this gift, empaths view the world very differently; they can feel even the most subtle of energy. An empath feels everything.

Empaths are incredibly intuitive and possess many natural psychic gifts. Unfortunately, they are often labeled by others as "too emotional" or "sensitive" and are often taught to suppress their gifts at a young age. This can lead to anxiety or issues around trusting in what they truly feel and experience.

Empaths are natural healers and can easily be identified. They are often the ones that friends or family members seek out when they need to "feel better." They are the sensitive ones, they are the old souls, who tend to be wise beyond their years, and they are the change makers and perspective shifters that the world needs right now.

If you have a young empath on your hands, they will be the kid always asking, "Why does it have to be that way?" and challenging your conditioned thought processes. You may find it frustrating at times, as these little old souls may try to parent you.

## What is an affirmation?

With a positive or self-empowering statement said out loud on a daily basis, you can begin to reprogram your mindset and shift your energetic output so it is based in love, rather than fear.

Daily affirmations are a simple yet effective way to fine-tune your subconscious mind. Saying affirmations on a continual basis helps to upgrade your thought patterns, leading you to align with more abundance. You can say these affirmations anywhere. Out loud or in your mind. While working out (my personal favorite), looking in the mirror, driving (another personal favorite), grocery shopping, or before dressing for a big event of some kind.

## How do I use this book?

This book has been designed to encourage you to follow your intuition. When you feel the need for guidance or sense your energy shifting, simply open the book and flip to any page. You will be delighted with just how perfect the message for you will be at that moment. There is no wrong way to do this, just feel your way through.

# AFFIRMATIONS

## It all starts with my heart.

One of the biggest lessons you must learn is to unlearn all of the things that at some point along your journey you have been conditioned to believe. It is crucial to come into the strong and unshakable knowing that you have all of the answers you need within you. Trust in and honor how you feel.

Honor the wisdom of the heart, and allow this wisdom to be the master. The key to ultimate abundance is to train the mind to be the tool that it is, so it can be in service to the heart's divine guidance. Empaths are blessed with the gift of deep intuitive knowing, and it is up to you to choose to harness and anchor this superpower.

## My intuition is for trusting, not rationalizing.

There will come a time on your journey when the mind will want to take over and do what it does best — question everything! Your mind will try to tell you that what you feel so strongly on an intuitive level isn't rational. The truth is, it isn't. Trust in what you feel anyway. Your mind will thank you later.

## I choose love.
## This is how I level up.

Love is hope, faith, excitement, positive expectation, optimism, freedom, empowerment, contentment, appreciation, happiness, and passion.

Fear is doubt, pessimism, frustration, impatience, worry, anger, hatred, jealousy, insecurity, unworthiness, blame, guilt, grief, and despair.

When you make the conscious decision to choose love over fear daily, you shift your mindset as well as your own energetic output, which helps you to align with a more fulfilling journey that is in service to your heart and your head.

# I am not a dime a dozen; I am a *diamond* within the dozen.

Oftentimes we sensitives, old souls, and empaths must be moved through the crucial lesson that we really are special. It's usually a soul lesson we set out for ourselves to learn. Unfortunately, this process typically comes with some heartbreak and will continue to repeat itself until we master the valuable lesson around self-worth.

Self-worth is all about learning to love yourself a little more, trust in your gifts a little more, raise the standards a little more, and simply recognize how truly rare you are. The right people will recognize this. The wrong people may never do so, or simply realize it too late. Either way, it doesn't matter as long as you recognize, love, and own your rarity.

## I am strong, I am capable, I am worthy.

Oftentimes, sensitive souls experience many situations, whether growing up or in early adult life, when their sense of self-worth takes a serious hit. Learning how to respect yourself, love yourself unconditionally, and ultimately, empower yourself is a lesson for every empath.

For empaths who have experienced abuse of any kind, this is an incredibly important affirmation to repeat daily until you absolutely, without a doubt *believe it!*

# I am worthy of abundance
# on all levels.

You just have to believe it.

# I am worthy of an equal energy exchange.

As an empath who has struggled for many years with setting boundaries, I understand how easy it can be to over-give at times in all relationships. Many disempowered empaths will find themselves giving and giving until their cup is totally drained.

When an empath is disempowered, they are total people pleasers, who simply find themselves wanting to do whatever they can to keep the peace with others, even at their own expense. This is unhealthy and is actually a trauma response that is typically learned at a young age or during a toxic situation.

Once an empath learns to love themselves as much as they love everyone else, everything shifts. If you find yourself in an unbalanced situation, repeat this affirmation as many times as needed. Energy exchange is a powerful thing, and it is important to make sure the amount of effort given by both parties is equal, healthy, and heart based.

I trust that there is a future
waiting for me that is beyond
what my logical mind is able
to grasp at this moment.

You are being guided to take that first step. It
doesn't matter how small or big it is. As you
continue to hold the intention of choosing love
and being true to you, you will be shown
multiple ways to align with abundance. The
universe will always support you, often in ways
you never would have thought possible.

# I am exactly where I am meant to be at this moment.

One of the most challenging things that intuitive empaths seem to battle is surrendering to the now, to this very moment. You may sense something coming or shifting for you and, at times, this can cause anxiety. It is important to slow down, take a deep breath, and accept where you are on your journey right now. Living in the past causes depression, and worrying about the future causes anxiety.

Remind yourself that every word, thought, and emotion you put out today creates your tomorrow. So, in this moment, surrender to the knowing that you are exactly where you are meant to be.

## I have always felt different because I am.

A perspective shifter, a change maker, an old soul, who came here to help create a new Earth. Honey, you were never meant to fit in. You think differently, you speak differently, you feel deeply, and you shine brightly for a reason. You are blessed and have a purpose, love. Own it.

# I allow my inner voice to be louder than the other voices around me.

You know what you came here to do. Do not deny yourself the opportunity to align with what you are meant to experience by listening to naysayers, those who cannot think outside their conditioned beliefs, or those too nervous to face their own wounding and healing.

Be brave enough to follow and carve out your own path. Let others watch and learn from you as you continuously choose love over fear.

# I honor my blueprint within.

Believe in destiny.

# I am love; love knows no bounds.

Love is the most powerful force in the universe,
and you are literally love incarnated, a
child of the universe with the ability to
cocreate anything your heart desires.

Challenge yourself to go beyond the limited
thoughts/patterns you have known thus far. Ask
yourself how far you would go if you knew you
had limitless possibilities and would be supported
every step of the way as you followed your heart
and continued to align with your true vibration.

# My story is my purpose.

We old souls, empaths, and sensitives more often than not get moved through more than the average Joe could ever handle. This is because we are strong enough to handle it, learn from it, and then, at some point on our journey, take that knowledge and use it to help others.

All of the experiences that you have had in your life thus far — even the not-so-fun stuff — have served a purpose. Whether this includes some sort of trauma or simply feeling as though you have never fit in or been understood, I promise there is a reason for all of it.

Challenge yourself to take a good, long, hard look at all of your chapters from a higher perspective. You will start to make sense of them and see that you've grown through all those experiences, which have taken you to this point. The point of aligning with your purpose. You never know, you may just start resonating with the term "wounded healer." ;)

# I believe because I choose to believe.

You do not need anyone to validate your beliefs.

## Spirit works through me.

There is always a reason for
everything you experience.

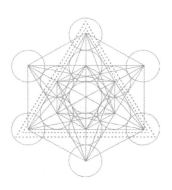

# My outer world is a direct reflection of my inner world.

As within, so without. Everything that is showing up in your physical world is a direct reflection of what is going on within you.

Take a good look at your belief system, your thought processes, all of it. Are you truly allowing yourself to live in alignment with abundance, or are you choosing to live in alignment with a lack mindset? Does this come from your childhood conditioning or life experiences? If so, why don't you begin to shift those beliefs right now?

In this very moment, start to believe that you are worth more than you are allowing. Start to believe that you deserve more abundance on every level, then get excited about it. See yourself living in alignment with more of what you really want, without restriction or reservations on "how it could happen."

When your energetic output matches your heart's true desires, you will begin to see the physical world rearrange itself for you. You will become an energetic match for the very things you desire.

So what do you really — in this moment — truly believe you are worthy of?

*Dream bigger.*

# I am an alchemist.

Albert Einstein said that energy cannot
be created or destroyed, it can only be
changed from one form to another.

We sensitives often take fear-based energy
and transmute it to love-based energy. This
is alchemy at its finest. Oftentimes we grow
through the harshest energies and situations
and then teach others how to do the same,
whether we are conscious of doing so or not.

The energy of fear and the energy of love
vibrate at different frequencies, and it is
through our intentions and conscious choices
that we can shift energy in our favor.

It's about believing and trusting that we are the
ones who always have the power to transmute
anything that happens to us or, should I say, for us.

# I am open to all possibilities
I allow myself to receive.

Let go of your expectations and how
you think things should be.

**My heart is the master, my brain is the tool to achieve what it desires.**

To achieve balance, train your mind to consistently surrender to the heart's instructions.

Reprogram your mind to be in service to the heart at all times. The heart leads, the mind must learn to surrender to its guidance.

# Fear is an illusion that I came here to conquer.

To overcome fear, you first have to feel it in order to realize that it is, in fact, an illusion.

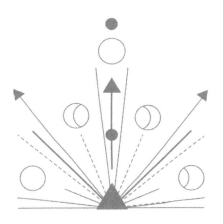

# I give myself permission to shine.

As much as you would like to help others and align with your mission/purpose from the comfort of your bedroom, you are meant to be seen, love.

I am sorry, darling, but you shine bright for a reason.

You are a light bearer, a way shower, and a soul on a mission.

You are meant to shine, baby, shine!

I need no external validation.
Everything I need to
know is within me.

*You* are the *key*.

I honor my body and its energy
levels. I listen to what it is trying
to communicate with me.

Take the time to check the energy of the people
you surround yourself with. It is important to
note how you feel around others. If something
feels off, there is a reason. If it feels bad
to be around someone, stay away.

At some point on your journey, you will encounter
or may already have encountered an energy
vampire. As sweet as you may be, you have
to set boundaries here. If someone is sucking
your energy, you will physically feel it.

## It's all good, I'm just shedding another layer.

We often build walls and create barriers to love. The awakening path is about shedding those walls and barriers so you can align with that higher vibration. When we are being moved through this process, we tend to leave behind people, places, situations, and things that are no longer in alignment with our highest good.

If you are feeling lonely or confused, know that in order to align with a higher vibration and attract more of what you desire, you have to let go of what is no longer meant for you. It has served its purpose. Be thankful for the lesson or experience.

You are simply letting go of the old, so new chapters can unfold. Stay positive, beautiful soul. You're leveling up again.

Something is waiting right around the corner.

## Clearing my energy allows me to see things from a higher perspective.

We are energetic beings, and every experience we encounter, whether positive or negative, leaves us with what I like to call energetic debris within our biofield. If you do not keep your energy/biofield clear, you become more susceptible to things like stress, anger, worry, doubt, and other lower vibrational energies. When this happens, you will feel a sense of not being grounded, and this can cause you to doubt your intuition or lose sight of the bigger picture of what may be really happening for you along your journey.

Being an energetically sensitive person, you must dedicate yourself to a lifestyle change and incorporate daily meditation, physical exercise, Reiki clearing, or any other practice that can help to ground your own energy as well as shift any energy that may come your way.

# Some people may refuse to see my light. Those aren't my people.

You have to learn to become so confident in who you are that when someone throws a projection or insecurity your way, it will not be able to shake you.

If someone refuses to see your light and decides to paint whatever belief they choose to have about you as a reality, let them have that belief. It is not worth the energy to try to make them see you.

When you become so confident in who you are that no one's opinion of you can shake you, the shift to claiming back your power will occur. It is important to remember that your transformation will make no sense to those who are not a part of your next level. Those who are meant to be a part of your leveling up will always see you for who you are and provide you with unconditional love and support. Those people *are your people*.

I bet those people already popped into your head while you were reading this, huh? Yeah, you know who they are. Those people right there, those are your soul besties.

# My emotions shape my reality.

Our emotions help shape our reality. When we feel good or think positively, we literally emit positive energy. When we feel bad or think negatively, we literally emit negative energy. Whatever energetic pattern we carry internally manifests itself externally.

We are made up of billions of atoms known as the building blocks of the universe. An atom is one of the smallest units of matter, made up of protons, neutrons, and electrons. When atoms are balanced, it's due to energy. What all this means is that human beings naturally create energy. Scientists now believe that energy stems from consciousness and that there is a direct connection between consciousness and the physical world.

So what does this mean in terms of aligning with what you want? Use your emotions wisely! When you are happy, you are in alignment. When you are on the opposite spectrum, you are not in alignment. Make the shift and know that the key to manifesting your desires is to become a vibrational match for those desires. What you desire is the key to aligning with your soul's journey. You desire what you do for a reason. You are meant to experience all of it. Believe this and align with love.

# My heart would never long for something I wasn't meant to experience.

Believe you are worthy of what it is that you truly desire. More often than not, we ask the universe for what we want, but we end up blocking it from coming due to our attachments/expectations of how it will arrive, or fears of not getting it at all.

Wherever it is that your heart is guiding you to go, honor that guidance and take the steps toward change. Surrender and allow the universe to transform you.

# Spirit is guiding me every step of the way.

As challenging as it can be to believe at times, you are never alone.

Whether it be through angel numbers (seeing repetitive numbers all over the place), synchronicity, recurring emotions/thoughts, or those intense moments of simply knowing, you are always being guided toward your highest path and being asked to choose love over fear. You have a spiritual team guiding you, and it is your responsibility to listen and be willing to receive the guidance.

## Overcoming self-doubt is a part of my journey.

The self-doubt that empaths, old souls, and sensitives experience is a part of the journey. How in the world are you ever going to learn to trust yourself if you aren't presented with opportunities to do so? Also, for those of you who are aligning with your purpose and feeling the call to serve in some way, how are you ever going to teach others how to do this unless you do it for yourself first?

To strengthen your intuition, overcome self-doubt, and align with what is meant for you, trust in what you feel rather than waiting for physical proof.

You will notice that the more you trust, take the steps, and really believe that everything happens for a reason, the more the universe shows up for you, often in ways that you would never expect.

Letting go of self-doubt is just another lesson in letting go of fear and a reminder that you are love, the most powerful force in the universe.

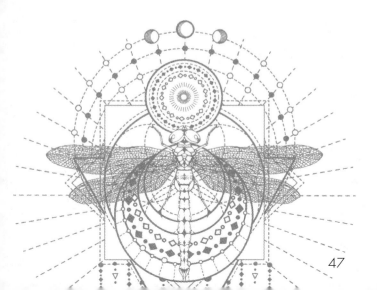

# I am my own damn guru.

It just takes a little bit of tuning into your own vibration, tapping into that heart, and voilà, you have the answers. It's about self-belief and trusting the process.

The moment you stop looking outside yourself, you will truly begin to own your power.

Gee, you are you.

## In order to embrace my divinity,
## I must first surrender to my humanity.

Accept your shadow. Your shadow is all the
not-so-fun parts of your personality. In order
to grow, you have to do shadow work.

This is how we level up and own our power. The
shadow is our human self, and it is through shadow
work that we are often reminded of our divinity.

Embrace it. Learn from it.

I let go of the limited beliefs that keep me from living in alignment with what I know is real.

Enough is enough. You feel the stirrings within — knowing change is meant to come or longing for change. It doesn't matter what society says or what other people may think.

*Go for it and trust in what you know.*

I release all that is no longer
serving me so I can align with
the abundance I am worthy of.

Let that lower vibrational, fear-based toxic shit go.

## Money is an energy source that flows through me.

Just like everything else in this world, money is simply energy, and unlike what many of us are conditioned to believe, there is plenty of it to go around.

Tap into this unlimited energy source, and allow it to flow through you!

Take a moment right now to check in with yourself. What are your true beliefs about money? How do you *feel* about money? Are you matching its abundance with love-based frequency, or are you repelling more of it from coming into your life by resenting and worrying about it?

I personally *love* money. I realized a few years ago, the more I amplified that feeling and the more I appreciated being able to pay my bills, afford bigger tips for people who waited on me, and purchase the items I desired without feeling guilt, the more of it I seemed to attract, often in unexpected ways.

What you spend time focusing on grows. Start shifting your beliefs about money, and watch how it begins to show up for you more.

# I choose to be the love that I desire.

We are vibrational beings. Whatever vibration we emit is what we will receive back. So if you desire to manifest a sacred partnership, you first have to become those very things you desire in a partner.

You must develop a healthy, loving relationship with yourself first. Loving the self unconditionally (flaws and all), not needing anyone or anything to validate you — this is how you align with more love. You must become an energetic match for it.

Sacred union begins within, when the heart and the head are in balance with one another.

# I give myself permission to grow and evolve.

Allow yourself the opportunity to venture into the unknown. When you surrender to the heart's guidance and trust your inner voice, the opportunity to really level up, grow, and evolve soon presents itself.

Allow yourself to take the leap, to listen to that call and trust where the universe is guiding you. You may surprise yourself once you realize just how powerful you are. The universe is waiting to present you with a new adventure and chapter to align with. Know that you are worthy of the growth and new experiences that are waiting and meant for you.

# It's okay to ask for help.

Despite what your badass warrior self
thinks, it is okay to ask for help.

Allow yourself to be supported. You do not have
to carry the weight of the world by yourself.

Every person who has ever leveled up has a
mentor or some sort of support. Talk to your soul
family or find a mentor or coach who understands
and will help empower you, support you,
and love you every single step of the way.

Let go of the idea that you have to do this alone
or that you will never find another who will
understand what you are being moved through.
Allow yourself to be surprised by who and what
can show up for you when you need it.

Soul family is very real, love. Let 'em
help you get to the next level.

# The journey isn't always about love and light. It's okay to lose my shit.

The awakening path to self-mastery is far from easy. This is the path of warriors, and there will be times when you wonder how much more you can take.

You do not have to hold it all together, all of the time. You are human. Take a deep breath, feel what needs to be felt, and then, when you are ready, make the conscious decision to shift that energy.

You will know what to do when the time comes.

Remember, the most chaos usually occurs right before you align with that which is meant for you.

# When I live in alignment with what my heart desires, I am fully supported by the universe.

When you are true to yourself, have pure intent, and choose love, you will be shocked at the opportunities delivered to you directly from the universe.

## When I make my own decisions, I move forward in my spiritual development.

Let go of the need to get everyone's approval or validation. No one knows or understands your journey the way you do. Every little part of your life has been perfectly designed for you, and you are the only one who knows what is right for you.

Many empaths often find themselves worried about what others will think or do as a result of the energetic shift a new scenario might cause.

Stand your ground, implement healthy boundaries, and keep facing your true north. You'll see, it will all fall into place.

After all, how will you ever build your intuitive muscles until you have had the opportunity to make your own decisions and trust in yourself?

## Instead of worrying, I choose to focus on what I desire.

I have yet to meet or work with an empath who isn't an overthinker. Empaths often feel the most subtle of shifts, and if they aren't grounded, this can cause excess worry or anxiety. This is especially true if change is naturally occurring in the empath's life.

It's important to learn how to separate yourself from negative thoughts that may occur. Challenge yourself to think of three things that are going well or three things that you are grateful for in your life the next time a negative thought occurs.

When you do this over time, the mind begins to reprogram, and you will notice that triggers become less powerful. Eventually, when a negative thought occurs, you will immediately counteract it with a positive one. You will begin to notice that instead of dwelling on what you do not want, you will focus on what you actually want to manifest.

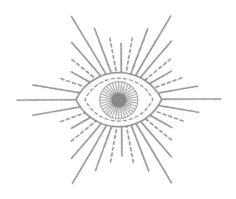

## I choose to do the work. I know it's up to me to move toward where I am being guided.

Among many things, feeling their way through things is one of the empath's many gifts. However, staying lost in the feels will get you nowhere. It is important to take the action steps that you are being guided to take so you can be a cocreator with the universe.

Empaths are incredibly psychic, and this superpower helps them align with abundance on every level. So when you experience multiple downloads (tons of ideas coming at you), intense feelings, and all-around aha moments and insights, do not dismiss or doubt this divine guidance as wishful or random thinking. You are receiving guidance on what steps to take next. *Do the work* and trust the process!

## I understand that fear is an opportunity for me to overcome myself.

Fear is the exact opposite vibration of what you are. But, you see, in order to overcome it, you must first experience it. This is how you begin the crucial lessons of learning to see through illusions and ultimately align with abundance.

## I know that everything happens for my highest good.

Every detour, every heartbreak, and every experience that seemed to knock you down over and over again happened to you for a reason. Sometimes it takes having to be knocked down lower than you have ever been in order to stand up taller than you were before.

Take a deep breath, love. Dust yourself off and *get back up*. You are a warrior, and you are on this journey because you are strong enough to conquer all that is thrown at you.

Every chapter has served a purpose. If one is closing, allow it to close and take a moment to really view things from a higher perspective.

What have you learned? Would you have been able to learn it and be where you are today had the experience not happened?

The goal here on this beautiful planet we call Earth? Soul growth and evolution.

## Everyone has their own journey to experience.

We cannot control the experiences that others choose for themselves. Everyone has their own path to walk. Let go of trying to save or heal others, and put that energy into your own journey.

If you feel something on an intuitive level with everything that you are and try to protect someone or "prevent" something from happening, save your energy and know that as hard as it can be, it is best to allow them to experience it. If you don't, you could literally be interrupting a soul lesson that they set out for themselves to learn.

Every one of us has a blueprint within, and the things that are meant to happen for our souls' evolution will eventually happen. It is up to each individual to learn the lesson being presented — or else keep repeating the pattern that is not serving them.

# Keep focusing on yourself and your own soul growth.

It's about being a way-shower, possibly even a catalyst of some kind, not someone who is constantly telling others what you feel or what you feel may be best for them (even if your intent is very pure). They will figure it out on their own, when the timing is right. If they ask for help, great. Show them love and never underestimate the power of planting a seed.

For intuitive empaths, this is a big lesson. You may feel something shift for others before they even feel it or experience it themselves. This could happen days, weeks, months, or even years before the event takes place. Allow others to learn on their own timeline.

I honor what I feel because I
know my emotions are the map
guiding me toward that which
I am meant to experience.

If you are happy, you are in alignment. Alignment
means being where you are meant to be. It
means abundance and happiness. When you are
unhappy, you are not in alignment, and something
needs to shift or change. Our emotions are the
map, the instructions, or guide, so to speak, that
we were all born with. Heed their guidance
(don't sulk in them), and then take action toward
aligning with a more fulfilling experience.

Our emotions are the indicator of what
serves us and what no longer serves us.
Trust in what you feel, and then level up by
choosing love over fear-based emotions.

Shift your energy, and shift the energy around you.

# I choose to focus on the now.

One of the most challenging things that we all seem to battle at some point is surrendering to the now, to this very moment. This is especially the case for intuitive empaths/sensitives. They may sense something coming or shifting for them and, at times, this can unfortunately cause anxiety.

Living in the past can cause depression, and worrying about the future can cause anxiety. Surrender to the now and make sure you remind yourself that every word, thought, and emotion you put out today creates your tomorrow. So take a deep breath and simply surrender to knowing that you are exactly where you are meant to be. There is a higher plan, and spirit is guiding you every step of the way.

# I understand that if I want abundance in my life, I have to first believe I am worthy of it.

If you want more abundance in your life, you must make the decision to start aligning with the vibration of abundance, which is love. This means removing fear-based thoughts, relationships, jobs, or any other situations that may be causing you to live in direct alignment with fear.

Take some time to journal or write out what fear-based energies need to be released in your life so you can start to align with what it is that you truly desire and are very much worthy of. Then, in a safe place, burn this list. If you enjoy intention-setting, you can even say something out loud to your spiritual team/the universe, such as, "Please take my fear and transmute it to love; I am now asking for your help to grow."

Send that energy out into the universe for transmutation. You will also be creating a physical anchored memory of consciously releasing what needs to be released, so if you later find yourself tempted to fall back into the same cycle that does not serve you, you can quickly remind yourself that you already released that energy, and you will remember that you have a choice to repeat the cycle or not.

## Boundaries are healthy, normal, and necessary.

Boundaries are essential to maintaining a healthy life. More often than not, empaths are people pleasers and have little to no boundaries set in place. If you have no boundaries set for yourself or accept constant violations, this can be a sign of low self-esteem.

Know your worth, love yourself as much as you love others, and know that when you set healthy boundaries for yourself, you are setting an example of how you expect others to treat you.

Remember, the only people who get upset when you set healthy boundaries for yourself are those who benefit from you not having any in the first place.

# Everything begins with intent.

Something I had to learn early on in my
spiritual journey was how to live intentionally.
What do you want to create, and what
is your intention around this creation?

When it comes to creating anything in your life,
take a moment to list intentions around what it is
that you truly desire. Use this as your foundation for
your creation; build upon it and lose anything that
is no longer in alignment with your true intentions.

Get in the habit of asking yourself, "What do
I want, and is this person, place, thing, or
situation in alignment with those intentions?
Is it an energetic match? Does it serve
me, and is it in service to my heart?"

# I honor my need for alone time.

We sensitives require alone time (often, we prefer it). It is crucial, and it is how we get back into alignment with our own vibration. Many people will be drawn toward the empath because empaths are natural healers and transmuters of negative energy. So, at times, you may notice everyone wanting or needing something from you. However, if you do not handle this properly, it can lead to what I like to call healer burnout and can actually harm you in the long run if you do not take the time to rebalance and ground your own energy field.

Alone time is healthy. Do not allow guilt or pressure from others to detour you from taking time for yourself. Fill your cup before filling that of others. The people who are meant to be in your life will understand.

# I inhale confidence and exhale doubt.

Sometimes you have to trust in what you feel, no matter how illogical it may seem. You feel the things you do for a reason. To feel so deeply is a gift. It is to be used for good, and once you trust and anchor this gift, you can consider it a superpower. Simply learn to take a deep breath and a leap of faith, and then trust in the path unfolding before you.

# I choose to give myself the love I have so freely given to others.

Empaths often battle with the tendency to give too much. This type of behavior usually has to do with the wounded inner child. Somehow, some way, they have been conditioned to believe that they have to give and give in order to receive love. This is a sign of codependency and can end up leading to energetic exhaustion, feelings of depression, and anxiety.

It is crucial to make sure your cup is full every day. Make it your daily intention to take care of the child within before tending to anyone else. What are they saying? What do they need?

Put your hand on your heart daily, tune in, and heed its guidance. In order for you to be the best version of yourself, it is important to remember that *you matter*.

# I choose to be an empowered empath.

Empowered empaths have strong boundaries, use their intuition and sensitivities as a strength, observe but do not absorb, and are master energy shifters.

Disempowered empaths have poor boundaries, are people pleasers, say yes to everyone, are walking emotional sponges, and can often pull the victim card.

Every day, you are presented with a choice. Choose empowerment.

## My words are vibrations.
## I choose them carefully.

The feelings, thoughts, and words we speak carry energy. When we feel good and think and speak positively, we emit positive energy. When we feel bad and think and speak negatively, we emit negative energy. Whatever energetic pattern we emit will manifest into our physical world. We are truly that powerful.

Make it your intention to choose positive words with your daily "I am," "I feel," and "I think" statements, and watch how much your thought patterns, daily experiences, and overall quality of life shift in your favor.

## I embrace my creativity and natural talents.

Know that you are naturally good at certain things for a reason. You are meant to align with all of the things that you love doing, experiencing, or expressing. That creativity and natural talent may be the very things that align you with your purpose.

Harness your gifts, use them, and allow yourself the opportunity to really see yourself and trust that these gifts are meant to serve you.

# When I feel triggered, it is an opportunity for me to heal.

You are being shown your shadow,
your own wounding.

Your issues can include anything from insecurity,
anger, or abandonment to low self-worth. It all
totally depends on what you are learning to heal
or master. Everyone's triggers are different.

We are simply mirrors of one another. The significant
people whom we attract into our lives tend to
mirror our issues back to us so we can recognize
and fix them for our higher good. From this higher
perspective, this is an incredible act of love.

Without judging yourself or others, keep
nurturing that child within and the healing
process will begin to occur naturally.

## Forgiveness is an opportunity to expand my consciousness.

One of the first things I felt when growing through my initial experience of awakening was a massive longing to forgive even those who'd hurt me the most. Holding onto anger, pain, resentment, and other fear-based emotions did nothing for me. It only held me back, held me down, and kept me from aligning with the vibration of abundance.

As your heart begins to open more, you'll begin to see the patterns and lessons that you and others must grow through. Anyone who has ever truly been moved through a spiritual awakening of any kind has most likely gone through this vital lesson.

The world is simply a school, and forgiveness is one of the many curricula we as souls come to experience. Forgiveness doesn't mean forgetting. It is simply releasing someone from an emotional debt that they owe you so that you can move forward and shed that layer of fear-based energy for good.

# I surrender the need to know how everything is going to happen.

Let go of destination addiction and have faith in the journey of self-discovery.

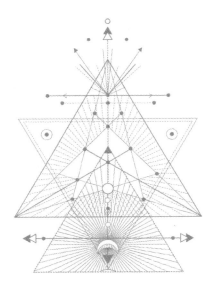

# The feeling of love quickens the flow of energy.

When we live in direct alignment with love, what we desire is attracted to us more quickly and we receive intuitive hits more clearly. Our natural psychic abilities strengthen to a degree that almost seems unfathomable to the human mind.

Love clears our biofield and our satellite receivers, so to speak, are able to receive divine messages loud and clear.

It's just about tuning in and finding that right frequency. Dial into 528 Hz, the frequency of love.

# When I ask the universe for something, I am always given the opportunity to align with what I am asking for.

Although we are usually never quite "given" the things we desire directly, we are often given the free will to make the choices to live in direct alignment with love (more abundance) or fear (less abundance and more pattern lessons).

## Doubt is the birthplace of faith.
## Fear is the birthplace of love.

You may not know exactly where you are
going and, at times, it may seem a bit
scary. But this is what cultivates faith.

Faith is the stepping-stone toward aligning
with more abundance on every level.

Walk by faith, take the steps to align with love,
and allow the universe to show you miracles.

# I choose to love myself the way I wish they did.

Love yourself a little more deeply and unconditionally. No matter the experiences or trauma you have been through, starting today, put that child within first before moving forward again.

Ask yourself daily if you are putting their needs first, and make a promise to cherish the guidance that comes through. When we begin to love ourselves the way we wish another had, the healing process can truly begin.

This is an excellent affirmation for anyone who has experienced abandonment, rejection, or trauma.

# My sensitivities are a gift.

Anyone can be cold. That takes no talent, but to feel and then use those emotions wisely to manifest abundance — now that, my love, is a gift.

# Spirit has my back.

Earth is simply a school, and we are mastering
lessons and curricula for our ultimate soul
growth. When you choose to trust in that inner
voice, do what you feel is right, and own
your journey, you are always supported.

Trust in the signs and the synchronicity happening
all around you. Let go of any doubt or worry.
You have a spiritual team supporting you,
encouraging you, and rooting for you to choose
love. The odds are in your favor for creating
miracles every time you do this. Keep going.

# I allow myself the opportunity to unlearn everything I thought I knew.

Do yourself a favor now, and put that ego/ mind in its place. Use it as the tool that it is.

You know nothing.

You are about to be shown everything. This is what happens when you align with love. Accept this now, and the path will become easier.

Congratulations, you are leveling up.

## My head is the tool to achieve what my heart wants.

Many of us have been trained since we were young children that the head is in charge, and it is best to always do the most logical thing. However, this often leads to a very disappointing and unfulfilling journey.

We have been living in a patriarchal society, programmed to believe for far too long that the desires of the heart are not to be trusted.

Your heart is the master and holds the sacred wisdom and instructions for you to align with your soul's journey. The head? It's the tool to help the heart achieve this.

Empaths, you have the biggest hearts around. Use this energy and strong gift of feeling deeply and wisely so you can manifest whatever reality you desire. Train your head to be in service to your heart, every time.

# Anger is healthy. It is the emotion that shows me where my boundaries have been violated.

Too many times we are taught that it is not okay to be angry. We have all had experiences when anger was not handled in a healthy way. Sensitive souls often do whatever we can to avoid this emotion and the possible abrupt energy shifts that can come with it.

Unlike what many of us have been conditioned to believe, all of our emotions serve a purpose, including anger. You do not have to stay caught up in anger, but you do have to feel it because like our other emotions, it is an indicator of what needs to shift or change.

It is okay to be angry at someone who has hurt
you or violated your boundaries in some way.
In order to heal anger, you have to feel it.

Do not allow anyone to gaslight you, manipulate
you, or make you feel guilty for feeling anger.
Anger is the inner child taking back their power.

# I choose to own my power.

If I had a dollar for every empath I have met who told me they are "so tired of feeling all the time" ... I understand how this can feel, but, honey, you were born with this gift to help heal yourself, others, and this planet.

To feel so deeply is a gift. The trick is to learn how to honor the emotions that arise and then shift what needs shifting on an energetic level. Anyone can be cold, be distant, and choose not to feel — that takes no talent. But to feel, honor, trust in your heart, and choose love — that's power.

Follow your heart, harness your gift, and be true to yourself. You are love incarnated, and love is the most powerful force in the universe. Own it.

I am attracted to other empaths,
intuitives, psychics, and healers
because I also have those gifts.

Like always attracts like. It is a universal
law; we attract the very thing we are.

You can spend years looking outside yourself for the
answers, but the truth is you have had the power
and answers all along. It's just been about choosing
and continuing to choose love. Love is the answer.
It is what activates and unlocks your natural gifts.

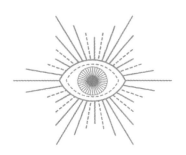

# My intuition knows her shit.

Trust that bitch.

# I am a limitless being who can manifest anything I desire into reality.

This affirmation is a favorite of mine. It is an incredible power statement for shifting your mindset almost immediately.

If you ever feel the opposite of this statement, visualize the outcome you actually desire and then make the conscious decision to shift, baby, shift.

As stated several times throughout this book, you are love, baby, and love knows no bounds.

It's about belief.

# I allow myself to be seen.

Many sensitive souls want to save the world from the comfort and safety of their shells. We typically have a very hard time being seen because we are usually very introverted. As a survival technique, we have always tried to blend in, even though (and we learn this as we get older) we were born to stand out.

However, most times, it is the soul not seeking attention who is the change maker. The soul who's been through the most holds the deepest wisdom. This is the soul who is here to help illuminate others and, ultimately, teach about love. This requires allowing yourself to be seen.

When I choose love, the universe
supports my every move.

Level up.

# It is safe for me to speak my truth.

There will be a moment on your journey
when you level up in such a way that you
will look back on it one day as the sensitive
soul that you are and say... "Wow."

This moment will happen when you begin to
speak your truth, to stand in your authenticity and
allow yourself to be heard. Unapologetically.

You feel everything you do for a reason.
Be your authentic self, no matter what.

If you are feeling the call to serve, speak your truth
and you will be supported. I promise. The right
people will flock to you, and the others who are
not meant for you will simply experience their own
journey in another place that is meant for them.

Many times, we sensitives struggle with speaking
our truth due to childhood wounding, when at
some point on our journey, our parents denied
our reality. Unfortunately, this leads us to feel

as though it is not safe to speak what is in our heart or live a life that is authentic to us.

The moment you choose to honor your blueprint without a parent or anyone else validating what you feel, you begin to heal.

If you are struggling to speak your truth in relationships, the longer you wait to express how you are feeling, the more uncomfortable you are going to become. This is a lesson around self-worth. It is important to speak up and expect your feelings to be honored and cherished.

Empaths, old souls, and sensitives often struggle with this lesson because it is typically a trauma response to something they have experienced or they simply do not want to hurt another's feelings or rock the boat in any way.

Hear me now when I say that the right ones will love you no matter what, and the ones who don't hear you are not meant for you.

# All that is for me flows into my life effortlessly.

There is no need to chase or worry about missing something that is meant for you, because everything that is meant for you to experience will flow your way.

It will be presented to you in some way — as an opportunity, as a smack in the face from the universe, or as a step-by-step revelation.

Attract what is meant for you.

Flow and grow.

## Actually, I can.

Stop denying what you are capable of.
Honey, you totally can. You've got this. Own it.

Despite what others allow me
to see, I know I feel what I
am feeling for a reason.

Trust your vibes. Vibes don't lie. Move forward.

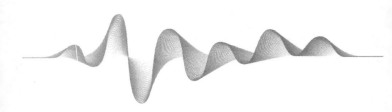

# I am intuitive. My gifts are so on the money, honey.

How many times have you said, "I knew it!" or "I wish I would have listened sooner"?

This affirmation is about trusting that first hit. *No second-guessing!*

# There is no reason to overthink the perfection of my soul's journey.

Everything you are being moved through
is by perfect design. Trust the process.

## Before I can help others, I must help myself.

This is a lesson many healers, sensitives, and empathic souls need to learn. You must move through experiences firsthand so you can ultimately help others awaken, recognize their own gifts, trust in themselves, and follow their own hearts.

You are allowed to be a masterpiece and a work in progress at the same time. As a healer, you may notice that you attract people who are a few months or years behind what you've been moved through. This is how spirit/the universe works through you. Work with and use what you know.

**Everything I see in my external world is a direct reflection of what I feel I am worthy of.**

Everything.

If you desire more, believe you are worth it and then take the steps needed to align with the abundance that is your birthright.

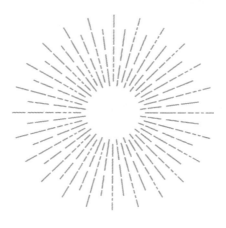

# When it comes to my spiritual journey…shh.

Beautiful soul, not everyone is going to understand what you are being moved through. In fact, more often than not, you may find yourself receiving lower vibrational energy from another when you speak about the clarity you are receiving or what you are thinking about aligning with.

Protect your ideas from others while they are developing. You are the one who truly knows what you are here to do. Take action as you are guided.

It may take a moment for others to truly see you, and that is okay. Stay facing your true north, surround yourself with those of like vibration, and keep training yourself to be more open to the divine.

# I am here for a reason.

This is no mistake or accident. You are reading this affirmation at this very moment because you are meant to. You have a purpose. Trust in what you are feeling, have always felt, and have always *known*: faith, love, and more faith.

Allow any transformation that
needs to occur to occur.

Think about all the chapters of your
story, from childhood to today.

You can't make this stuff up. It has
all happened for a *reason*.

Victory is here for you. *Align* with it.

# Nighttime is my power time.

Highly intuitive, empathic, and sensitive
souls often find themselves tapping into and
tuning into their gifts more at nighttime. This
usually has to do with the fact that the energy
around them is calmer and less scattered.

Creativity is usually at an all-time high
for sensitive souls during this time.

Despite what others feel your schedule "should
be," if you find yourself wanting to be more
creative during this time, there is a reason for it.

Many soulpreneurs and creatives find
themselves being on a completely different
time schedule than others, and this is okay.

This is your playground; you make the rules.

# A broken heart is an open heart.

Let me tell you, beautiful soul, a broken heart is something I have certainly experienced.

I have come to realize that a broken heart is the catalyst, a pattern that will keep repeating until it is fully healed.

To have your heart broken is the opportunity to have it broken wide open. You may not see it that way in this moment, but that perspective shift will come through one day. I promise.

You see, when your heart has been "broken," you are being given the opportunity to heal your own shadow and become whole again. Not seeking anything outside yourself from another, you learn to love yourself as much as you love another, and this love is *golden*!

When your heart is truly open, you learn
that love is an energy that you embody
and what *you* really are is limitless, free,
unconditional, and without attachment.

A broken heart is the catalyst for learning all
the painful yet crucial lessons on the path to
enlightenment, self-discovery, and soul growth.

Feel it for as long as needed. Shift it when you
can and see it for what it is teaching you. Those
emotions are messengers. If you truly love someone,
that will never go away. You are simply learning
that it is love that lifts you up to where you ultimately
belong, however the lessons tend to come through.

I promise, you are not broken, and one day
it simply will not hurt as much anymore.

**My soul family shows up for me just as I am leveling up on my journey.**

You will be amazed at who shows up in your life, just as you need them to help you through your next transition and growth period. The key is to open your heart, choose love, and allow new experiences in. Your soul family will always show up for you. The higher you rise, the more you align with them.

Everyone is awakening; we all just seem to notice at different points on our journey.

Allow others the opportunity to experience their lessons, just as they are meant to.

# My heart is a direct reflection of God.

If you feel it so deeply within your heart, how could it be wrong? When you have a direct line to the CEO, so to speak, why would you mess around with the third-floor receptionist?

Despite what you have been conditioned to believe, your heart is the only approval and validation you need to move forward. Follow your blueprint. Not everyone will understand, and that is okay.

It is so important for you to follow your own heart. Know that everything is within you. Allow yourself to start and then continue using your natural intuitive gifts.

Challenge yourself to let go of what you can see or prove, and then you will be able to *feel* what is right. The heart always knows.

# Depression comes from lack of expression.

I haven't worked with one empath or sensitive soul who hasn't suffered from depression. What I have found on my own journey is that depression comes when you are not expressing yourself in some way or allowing yourself to stand in your authenticity.

Everyone needs to be able to express themselves in some way, whether it is through a creative endeavor or simply by speaking up or speaking their truth. It is necessary for soul growth and development.

For those of you who feel the need to express yourselves creatively, remember you are drawn toward what you are passionate about for a reason. Allow yourself to simply *be you*.

# I am a manifesting junkie.

What do you want to create? What do you want your physical world to look like six months from now? A year from now? It is time to get creative and put that imagination to good use!

Every little bit of energy you put out today creates your tomorrow! Why not have fun with this knowing and become a conscious creator with your life?

Believe you are worthy of your desires, and watch how quickly the universe will hand you opportunities to align with those very desires.

# Analysis is paralysis.

It's time to get out of your head and back into your heart. Feel your way through the situation, then take action! If you are receiving divinely inspired ideas, it is crucial that you move toward where you are being guided to go so opportunities are not missed.

Use that mind as a tool in service to the heart. Do not allow the situation to become stagnant because you overthink or have an illusion that perfection can be attained.

Succeeding takes starting with a clear intention, commitment to your purpose, and a willingness to stay the course until you have aligned with your goal.

# It's okay to let go.

Too many times we sensitive souls find ourselves caught up in situations or cycles that simply no longer serve us. These could be related to limited thought patterns, inner child wounding, attachments, or because, for some reason, we feel we can save or fix something that cannot be saved.

Oftentimes the lesson you are meant to learn in these situations is to let go and trust that you are being guided to align with something better suited for you and more in service to your heart.

When it is time to let go of something or someone who is no longer in service to your heart, visualize a rearview mirror with a sign saying, You're Not Going That Way.

Once you begin the transformation process, there is no looking back. There is no need to look at the old version of yourself. Instead, focus on moving forward and tapping into an ever-evolving, more brilliant version of your fullest potential.

## I am worthy of sacred partnership.

Believe it in order to receive it. The moment you come into balance with yourself and achieve sacred union within, a sacred partnership will then begin to manifest externally as well.

Too many times we deny ourselves the abundance that we crave when it comes to partnership. We settle for less than we deserve because we have been conditioned to believe that we do not deserve the very thing we desire.

The truth is, you desire the very things you do out of a relationship because you are meant to align with them. It is simply about loving yourself enough to stop aligning with fear and start choosing love.

# Others' inability to truly see me has nothing to do with my worth.

Honey, let 'em think what they want to. You have *shit* to accomplish.

# The right connections will have me falling back in love with myself.

No drama. No games. No fear.

*Straight empowerment.*

Every relationship serves a purpose for your soul growth, and that is a very beautiful thing. But when the relationship has served its purpose, allow yourself to be brave enough to open your heart, see things from a higher perspective, send them love, and then let them go.

Surround yourself with those who want to see you succeed and will push you to see how truly bright you shine.

# The more I choose love, the stronger my intuition and natural psychic gifts become.

Spirit dwells in the high vibrational energy of love. The more you dwell where spirit dwells and align with your true vibration, the stronger your gifts become.

It is about, yet again, choosing love over fear. Daily.

When you harness the energy of love, clarity and insight always come. When you allow yourself to get distracted by and dwell in fear, spirit cannot get through to you.

Think of yourself as a radio. You have to tune into the right station before you can receive its messages. That station/frequency is love.

## I am ready and open to allowing new experiences into my life.

So, you think everything has to flow in your life
according to the plan you have created?

Save yourself the time and worry now.
Throw those plans out the window, love.

Allow yourself the opportunity to experience
something totally unexpected and new.

You may just discover that you wanted
something you never knew you did.

It is possible to love again.

Open your heart.

I know I make the best possible
decisions I can with the information
I have in those moments.

Don't second-guess yourself, beautiful soul.
You did and are doing exactly what you're
supposed to do. You are exactly where you
are meant to be in this very moment.

Trust your heart and have faith in
your intuitive knowing.

# I create my own reality.

Own your power.

# I am a master energy shifter.

It is important to harness and honor your sensitivities, but it is also crucial to understand that your emotions are simply messengers. These messengers are letting you know what needs to stay, shift, or change.

When you find yourself being triggered by lower vibrational energy, that is fine and normal. We live on a planet where we are consistently being given opportunities to be triggered. However, it is important to shift that energy as soon as possible by making the conscious decision to do something that makes you feel good.

This shifts your energetic output and helps you align with a more abundant manifestation process.

When you make the daily choice to choose love over fear, you slowly begin to upgrade the default autopilot program you are running on. An upgrade, so to speak, begins to happen.

When this happens, you shift the signal you are emitting to the universe and can begin to see a more positive, abundant experience show up for you.

The physical external world is simply an illusion, and it can change at any moment when you choose to shift the energy you are allowing in and emitting out.

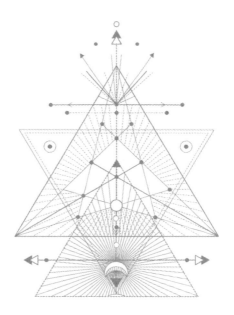

## Feel first, then act.

Allow your heart to lead you. Feel first before
you make any decision, then, once you have
clarity on what your emotions are trying to
communicate with you, take action based on
what your heart wants to achieve or experience.

# I allow myself the opportunity to be vulnerable.

When you allow yourself to just be who you are, you own your story (ugly parts and all) and embrace your silly, goofy, emotional, and passionate self.

You harness the power to change lives, shift perspectives, and align with even more abundance.

# My past does not define me.

Whatever you have been moved through,
challenge yourself to look through the experience
and see it for what it was — a lesson of some
kind. Then take that lesson and transmute
the experience by turning it into love.

## I choose the path that I know is meant for me.

Only you know what you are here to do and what is yours to experience. Follow your heart.

## Love that has to be hidden isn't true at all.

Stop looking at the connection you may have with someone through rose-colored glasses. If you have to hide them, if they have to hide you, if you have to hide who you truly are or what you truly desire, or if they have to do the same, then one or both parties are not being true to themselves or any other people who may be involved. This holds back ALL parties from their own soul lessons, karma, and ultimate evolution.

Love is friendship that has been set on fire. Marry or be with your best friend, but don't confuse attachment with friendship or love. That's just comfort and patterns that need to be healed playing out. Real friends (every relationship needs friendship before they can be lovers) call you out on your own bullshit, push you to be your best self, allow you to have your own truths, love you unconditionally, and will share you and your victories with the world. That's love. Choose that.

# It was not my fault.

*A special affirmation for my fellow sensitive souls who've experienced child abuse.*

It was not your fault, it never was. You were a kid.

You are good enough. You are special.
You are worthy of abundance and of
everything your heart desires.

You simply mirrored to your abusers what
they needed to heal within themselves.

If you are still being moved through the
healing experience, know this: We are all
souls. We all have lessons to learn, and
this place is simply a school to do that.

Allow the forgiveness process to unfold.

Reparenting myself has been one of the best
experiences I could have ever moved through,
because it has helped align me with my purpose.
It has helped me learn how to tune into my own

vibration and honor who I *am* without needing approval from anyone else. It has helped me realize how truly powerful of a soul I am and, to this day, I am thankful for it all. Without all of my experiences, I would not be who I am today, and I love the hell out of myself — the woman I have been and the woman I am becoming.

You cannot change the past, but you can change your perspective on it.

It all starts with your mindset, with your thoughts and the words you say to yourself every day.

Keep growing, you powerful warrior. There are new chapters unfolding.

# I let go of the attachment
# to my trauma.

There are situations in our lives that can be quite devastating and although they require time and sometimes professional help to heal, we don't have to keep re-living the trauma or pattern over and over again. It's an old story that can keep you caught in a loop, unable to create a new chapter.

If you have experienced some trauma on your journey, it does not define you and it is no longer a part of your daily journey unless you allow it to be.

Allow yourself the opportunity to experience something new. Let yourself create and align with a new story and new thought patterns.

Allow yourself the opportunity to live in the now. When you do this, it creates new energy that allows new experiences and new patterns to unfold.

# ABOUT THE AUTHOR

**Stephanie Jameson** is an intuitive empath, a psychic medium, an author, and a certified Reiki master. She works with individuals all over the world who find themselves being moved through the awakening journey, including some who are discovering that they themselves also have light working gifts to share. She understands that that separation from others or from spirit is simply an illusion.

Stephanie also understands the struggles that come along with being an energetically sensitive person. She knows that she was moved through these experiences firsthand so she could ultimately help others recognize their own gifts and trust in themselves. Nothing brings Stephanie more joy than helping others find peace, clarity, and healing. For more information, you can visit www.divinesouljourney.net.